I & We

I & We

Poems by Joseph P. Wood

CW Books

Published by CW Books
P.O. Box 541106
Cincinnati, OH 45254-1106

ISBN: 9781936370115
LCCN: 2010938180

Poetry Editor: Kevin Walzer
Business Editor: Lori Jareo

Visit us on the web at www.readcwbooks.com

Acknowledgements

I wish to thank the editors of the following magazines where these poems first appeared, sometimes in a different version and occasionally with a different title: 5 A.M., 32 Poems, Beloit Poetry Journal, can we have our ball back, The Canary, EOAGH, Elixir, Exquisite Corpse, Faultline, Good Foot, Gulf Coast, Indiana Review, Madison Review, MARGIE, Passages North, Phoebe, Poet Lore, Prairie Schooner, Quarter After Eight, Rattle, RHINO, River City, Salt Hill, Soundings East, Sycamore Review, Terminus, Texas Review, Verse Daily, and West Branch.

Some of these poems also appear in the chapbook In What I Have Done & In What I Have Failed to Do, Elixir Press.

I also wish to thank the Djerassi Resident Artist's Program for the time and space to work on this manuscript.

Thank you to Jason Thompson, Spring Ulmer, Julian Billups, Nora Mitchell, and Michelle Warner whose insights helped shape this manuscript.

Thank you to Mike, Jane, Jim, and Kim Godsoe for their company.

Thank you to both my U of A communities.

Most of all, thank you to Amy whose patience, love, and faith sustain me every day.

Table of Contents

But if all our losses are a mirror
In which we see ourselves advance,
I believe in its terrible, empty reflection,
Its progress from judgment toward compassion.

Jon Anderson, "A Commitment".

I.

In What I Have Done & What I Have Failed to Do

What I would give to be a blip without a name.
As it is, I am an American.
                                        I am the photographer
snapping The Cross submerged in my urine;
I am the doublespeak that makes this picture valid.

Why is a question whose sum-total is useful
as a cardboard junk launched down the Mississippi.
My leader urges *row, row.*
                                        His words repeat
like so much heartburn. I never thought God
would snap my spine.

A Half-Century Contemplating the Double Helix

The blind man wants to make love
　　　　　　to the deaf man's sister
so the baby will know two senses
　　　　　　of loss. Outside the hospital,
the poplars radiate exhaust
　　　　　　& our squirrels chatter like engines.
Our books all smell like a theory
　　　　　　of objects forever crashing
upon the hollow bottoms of clouds
　　　　　　& the clouds' only objection
is that the rain confesses nothing.
　　　　　　Presidents stand among the congress
of redwoods swearing the years
　　　　　　can be photosynthesized, that light
is only as good as its desires:
　　　　　　the hawk's zooming eye,
the red beak of the relay tower
　　　　　　slurping away at the airplanes
as sleek as frozen embryos.
　　　　　　The dawn cracks a new orange.
The orange is the old orange
　　　　　　perhaps without the crimson
of ambulances just this once.
　　　　　　An old man watches
the rowers break the river
　　　　　　into a thousand units of time
so new the old man will die
　　　　　　or be young again—we speak to him
as if to the pinpoints of stars
　　　　　　brittle enough they threaten
to confetti our skylines
　　　　　　before rendering darkness.
We think of darkness.
　　　　　　Quite a bit.
We think of it as a cave
　　　　　　where our babies were fugitives
from the sun until the sun
　　　　　　exploded itself, each spot a turtle

extracted from its shell
                & blown across the galaxy like this.

Our Luck

The road was a slot machine turned off for the night.

Pittsburgh was the line snorted back in Columbus.

The new sun hurt the skyscrapers in a way

I only thought a baby could be hurt by its mother:

It wanted to eat the hearts of the window washers

Dangling from what can only be coined as The Stupidest Faith.

During my days of faith, I had watched the elderly

March off to the community center for a morning

Of water aerobics & a game of *Who has the longest*

Memory? They marched so as not to be smitten

With their remaining time. How is it I'm not thirty

But feel drowsy when watching the anemic starlight

Hit the land, the wind, some distant water tower

Spray painted with *If I can't love you, I'll kill you.*

We're all so predictable we're ominous. Why can't

Our souls be paper plates carried off by ants,

Corn on the cob left to decompose in the sun?

If it rained, it rained, & we would finger the dice

Believing we had won.

Facts

When I was child, I believed
Germans had three breasts
or Spaniards penises
that looked like question marks:

if the sixth grade genius said it was so
then yeah...Then in third grade
Frau Krull arrived like a wounded whale,
& that exotic lie yawned before us.

If we couldn't trust the sixth grade,
what to make of the seventh
who insisted pot fizzled & popped
your brain cells *in fun ways.*

Who was it that schlepped down an alley
to find our stutterbox Jon Armstrong
spraying his puke with the gutter,
the distant sound of older, spacey laughter...

Frau Krull left next year
to have a baby with two eyes,
one mouth. *How boring* we thought
until we heard its skin was clear

as spring roll wrappers. *It's because
she's a Nazi,* the genius told us,
God's a Jew. God loves a good joke,
the seventh grade said, *would you care*

for a Whip-it? How these kids mutated
into law partners, garbage collectors,
PTA members is beyond me. All I know
is that they spread the country

like an infinite thistle-grass
& the less-fortunate are its mulch.
I hate my Dad, Armstrong once yelled,
if only I could shoot him. Later that year,

a steamroller flattened the man.
The baby, of course, had organs
that twisted like European borders.
Krull did what Krull did: move & blend

with some other population. *Will they know
her truth*, we asked ourselves. *Who cares!*
a boy yelled. He was tall & swift & smelled
of alpine meadows, of airplane seats,

& we flocked toward him, our droll personas
split like plaster, but today, over that hill,
gnarled oaks, threadbare pine, & fingers
of granite that punctuate the dusk.

Below the Saw Blade

Buried in Tuesday's *New York Times*: a man,
drunk & bumbling, & the saw blade doing
what a saw blade should be doing: adios

rock climbing, saxaphoning, & walking
five dogs at once—even the docile ones
need restraining, such as it was yesterday

at a Bay Area dog park, where a corpse,
beheaded & pregnant, lay on the shoreline,
& the greyhounds were held back from

what they love to do: sniff, lick, scratch
the swollen belly with such curiosity
that a grander horror might come to pass:

the baby, or rather, the corpse of baby
spills out onto the sand: ten formed fingers,
curled toes, smaller, yes, nonetheless alike

the dozens of nuns left to rot, jungle-deep,
1980s, throats slashed & tongues pulled
out through the slits: Colombian neckties

it's crudely referred to, but perhaps crudity
is the correct path up the mountain:
the crucified hundreds, if they were men,

always on a hill's apex, were not given
loincloths, but rather, their penises, due
to blood flow restriction, body's position,

were always erect, & most, even in throes
of blinding pain, would blush & beg to hide
themselves: or so it was told by an aging

priest, Friday, over Merlot, rice, & trout—
the fish, struggling against the water, saw
the hook's milky glint, & in one swift gulp, bit.

Sheep

When the first plane hit the tower,
a good friend, in lower Manhattan,
was jerking off in a janitor's closet.
He lived for indiscretion
as the saints lived for God,
but unlike them, never got nailed:
after almost impaling himself
on a broom, my friend stumbled
to the first floor, got the gist,
& fled thirty blocks Queens,
watching people disperse,
ants whose hole was trodden—

except a fleet of priests
marching toward siren flares,
huge clouds of dust—my friend
would deduce the next day—to administer
Last Rites. To see this herd was
to believe each lugged
the boroughs' sins like a yak
yoked to a 15th century oxcart.
A Medieval Studies major,
my friend had loved to ramble
on Europe's founding: glumness:

A child, exhausted from digging
a hole where his sister would be
laid, trips across a rat, its fleas—
might as well pitchfork his heart,
my friend guffawed, rubbing
his hands over some imagined flame,
& to think, his parents were giving
the time to some wheat-starved farm-hand,
blue buboes on all their inner thighs...

I can't tell you what became my friend.
He joked about Battery Park housing values
before moving West, with a wife & little

mouths of responsibility…Sometimes his cocky,
sidelong grin arrives like a lighthouse
beyond my sleep—here are the flames,
here the dust, I shall follow & wake.

Our History, Chapter V: "War Brewing"

They hired armed guards because there was no drink.
They were the finest tavern in the municipality, &
only ten Shekels or Euros per guard, machine gun or
bayonet, it was a deal none-too-soon. The piers
snapped with so many cracks the docked junks
groaned as the SS Enemy Tanker pulled in. The
ensigns, orderly as crew cuts, disembarked to the
square for a night of loosey-goosey prostitution,
though later, lathering their Viking beards, mere boys
quipped *snatch.*

Snatch was that period's vicious word. *Gaping* the
adjectival pistol. *Snatch* & *Gaping,* peasant brothers,
gunned down Archduke Voodoo Allah. Before the
firing squad they quivered, *we done thought he was a
boar; we were weak with hunger.* They weren't unique.
Like many of that era, flags pasted on the tanks' sides,
they shot their respective obscenities, as free men,
from the confines of their huts.

Then typhus hit.

Babies wailed through the night while mothers shook
their fists at their ceilings. Fathers' eyes sunk in the
morning, only to find their bosses in Windsor ties
slumped on slab desks of marble, expired. Naturally,
the town bakeries boarded up. The headlines
proclaimed the tribal constable was in cahoots with
plague fleas.

Down by the skyscraper, abutting the moat, men the
color of a plastic army took to the streets. The names
of the streets sounded like bamboo shoots. Like a
blow dart whizzing by an explorer's ear. Mothers
hunched to the parched ground, in this photograph,
as if to a railroad of baby bones. The train could be
decades away.

If One is Wise He is a Traveler; If Foolish an Exile

—In honor of Johannes Kelpius, Philadelphia's first known mystic

Your body was to ascend your death.
Your casket tossed into the Wissahickon.
When the splintered hickory box lay on the banks,
Your corpse went upright & emanated lightning—

Or so the story goes. This was the 17th century.
You & your disciples huddled a shale cave;
The Wilderness Woman never did rapture you.
And now your celibacy is buried beneath

Your dwelling's dirt floor—itself obstructed
By broken glass, condom wrappers, little bags
Emptied of coke? I wish a ship
did not beget a ship, a settler a settler:

We're field mice to owls, Dear Johannes.
The sun is not raiment we share.
The creek grows browner by the hour
As the hickory box splinters the banks...

A Brief History of a River Ward Row Home

Forget the masterpieces of nothing except extravagance. Let the suburbs keep their dumb waiters & expansive Doric porches. In my Umbrian façade covered with ivy, I was a triumph of simplicity —all our humble vessels were...

Then the river filled with offal. Then the smog was held aloft by street lamps. The trolley took the able-bodied from us, & the able-bodied spent the day knee-deep in yarn.

Of course the mills would come to empty themselves like a corpse's orifice. The taverns shrunk the humans into bloated fire ants, who scattered the tavern as the sun rose...

Sharp winter stars. Anemic light. Faint pulse through the roof rot, the hobos, half-chewed scrapple.

August's Diary

Summer: season for loathing. Everyone smells of death & the dead simply fry. Or Welcome to the unemployment office where the temperature is so pleasant it must be a spaceship. The leader has some type of rod in her hand that will determine your future. *Have you looked for work this week? Did you receive any money?* But everyone here must be human because dread flows freely like air. There's about fourteen different languages going at once, all revolving around the approximate time for the bus back home. It's a bus that asks for your femur in place of money. It's a bus where the seats are made of brain scar tissue. Why else would this woman in a Dorothy-&-Toto pink dress keep punching herself in her head while drooling a river? What you need now is water. But no, there's only this semi-angel, no bigger than a dust mite, fluttering on your shoulder & chiding *hey buddy, I recommend this teach you something other than fear.* Your reflection against the window is washed with some type of dusk that's on the verge of nuclear. Cockroaches & K-Rations & skin falling off like cocktail dresses come to mind.

Luxor by Luxor

On KTKT AM 990, The Voice of True Nevadans, Burt Lee growls *we
    shall not be deterred by kamikazes, cutthroats, & cowards...*

And somewhere, in this desert metropolis, where the people reek of
    grief, a mailbox is exploding

For amusement. And may I say these times amuse

The way lions amused the Ancients, those beasts' pompom tails & go
    get'em attitude.

I'm beginning to see the value of pompoms,

I'm beginning to want a well-manicured field, the goal posts glittering
    on the horizon

And the block-head blocker fullback to be raised in praise of his
    beautiful, mediocre abilities.

Lately, who wouldn't cast a suspicious eye

On the mere, predictable sublime: the time I rappelled

Into a pool was bejeweled with monkey ferns & skittish trout

And I put my head beneath the Caribbean-like water & heard the
    women sing

*Go to sleep little babe Go to sleep little babe Momma & me & the devil make
    three...*

However, these days, this casino is pumping in quarts of oxygen

By the minute, it's 5 a.m. & my babies are dead

Asleep at my feet while I get reacquainted with the sound of jackpot

Happiness, the blackjack dealer mysteriously stroking his goatee...

I step outside the Luxor, less burdened by coin, to smoke a Kool

Under one of the most milquetoast sunrises. I look up

At this pyramid of glass only Vegas could build

And consider how the Egyptians whipped the crap out of the Jews.

And how should I feel knowing one night, a whole fleet of the chosen

Jumped from one of those seven wonders & splashed

Into each other's blood hundreds of feet below

And their last collective thought was *In this motion we have never*

Felt so alive. And you, my citizens, surely you know the name of

The game is luck, & here is our hand, don't be afraid,

You can smell our success smolder across our brain-gray globe.

From Nowhere to Nowhere

Rain, the most brilliant hippie scholar I know, says no
one thinks about Philadelphia anymore: New York &
DC engulf poor little Baltimore & you. Of course, she
adds, MOVE had you back on the map for a while. I
can still hear the school bus chorus: *The roof, the roof,
the roof is on fire, we don't need no water let the
motherfuckers burn.* I sang it too, a fifth grader, on my
way to school where Sister Steven would inform the
class it's a sin to wish death on anything· God loves
all his animals.

What makes a human human, Sister Helen posited a
year later in Life Sciences, is his ability to reason, &
this she said, as my hands tried to go beneath Sally
James plaid skirt, her desktop concealing my
movements I thought, makes us moral. After
detention, I watched Ramona Africa paraded before
the news cameras as she held up her hands cuffed
together. That year, Osage Avenue was being rebuilt
—our mayor's apology for torching 70 odd houses.
Not on my dime, my father would complain, beer
firmly in hand, *those monkeys can use their own welfare
checks to pay for it.*

Sally James had mayonnaise-colored knees, & much
later, during a college winter recess (I was living in
the vast, blank Midwest now), when I ran into her on
the street, the first time she spoke to me since the
"touch thing", she said she was not doing so hot: the
Lupus she had since childhood had weakened her
substantially & all she wanted was to get a little color
in her skin—*You know, look normal to the guys at the
Community College.*

We were on a commercial stretch of road which, like
the rest of our neighborhood, was being gentrified, &
in place of the old Poles really starting to fill the
graveyard were mostly college kids renting on their

parents' coin. My father didn't seem to mind. He converted to Pentecostal & began to speak in tongues in his own front yard. I watched with something someone might call horror if it weren't such an overused & thus meaningless word.

Why did I feel this way? My father was alive & clapping & singing each Sunday sandwiched between two black families who, coincidentally, moved from the Southwest suburbs—Drexel Hill, Wawa, Swarthmore (names which, to me, invoke a nose in the air)—to homes three blocks from where my father lived. It was 1995. The nuns were gone by now. Some of MOVE had been dead awhile. But the downtown was sprucing up, & there were more parades.

I went to one of these parades. People were waving flags as brainlessly as they breathed. A motorcade of ancient vets went by & some of them wore little fezzes. Although I had (& have) never been there, I thought of Turkey, a country whose feet are in two continents. Rain has been to Turkey. She believes it's more accurate to say that the nation is ripped by two continents. Everyone looks more or less the same outside the cities, she says, because they're all poor as dirt.

II.

Via Her Body, I Discover where I'm Not

The foldout tables for lunch at the rally
had American flags taped upside-down
& pictures of Bush with X's through them.
I was confused: our purpose?:
                                    to protect

some rare breed of cedar
or the rarer jay that nested in it—

I came for the women:
One in a sundress dizzy with paisley prints
leg hair thick & wavy. I edged up to her
beside the buffet table, an assortment
of tofu turkey, succotash, four varieties of couscous,
& enough *After the Falls* juices to make a river.
She was with her friends, all of whom were ragging
on some absent, forever flaky member

but my love held a long silence,
& I pictured falling into her pause
as if into a bed of clover.
                          The wind kicked up.
Propane burners snuffed out. Everyone's hair was blown except for
my new wife, her skin a monument to anemic luminance.

So why did my right hand start to tremble
& saliva foamed at my mouth like a bull?
People were frowning because it made them
think of lobster bibs dotted with blood, the smell
of newly oiled machines, some eviscerating, separating
cow or pig organs. This was the type of factory
forever festooned with fog, whose cold, concrete floor
made one think of Soviet-era architecture...

Outside this plant, my love was a yak.
Explosions approached.
Throngs of people whose clothes looked chewed
yammered to God for bread.
In knee-deep mud, I apologized: everyone's face

jaundice. And the shrapnel began like rain.

My yak was now a moose. My moose now a thigh.
And why were my fingers serrated?
And why did I bring my right hand down?

April, April, April: little whore, you never did come.

The Punch

Murphy's left cross grazed my cheek;
I came back with an upper cut.
Our faces swelled red when the nuns
broke us up; we were friends
in two hours. In the ring,
everyone's a friend because anyone
can take down anyone. A nose breaks,
a vessel bursts; you stung like a bee,
but now the bee stings you   your wife
towels off your drool. Remember that
game, not in the ring, but on the court
when a gangly Kermit Washington
coldcocked Rudy Tomjanavich?
Tomjanavich said when he awoke
he thought the scoreboard fell
on his head! There was a metal taste:
spinal fluid leaking into his throat—
if the punch has grace it's the grace
of discovering the bones can bend.
If the punch has doom it's the doom
of discovering the bones can't bend
enough. Your wife towels off your drool
& your brains says *Friday, it's fish.*
Your wife says, *here, drink this,*
& sends you off to sleep. Some nights
I thought the stars were made just so
I could rattle my fists over them.
Some nights the stars were paler
than malaria. Kermit Washington
auctioned his Porche for a tank
of drugs to save an African village.
Rudy T took drugs because he awoke
in a sweat from sleep: the fist
was as big as basketball, coming, coming
closer; he went to duck, but no.

Total: A Biography

In order to experience the shooting pains
of Uncle Hymie's sciatica, you must know

a lifetime of newspapers slung in a satchel
& the smudge of Russian left on his hands

daily. Calculate then the exact amount of lye
lathered into his palms beneath the faucet,

& compose a ratio of toxin to skin. When
perfect, then speculate his maximum longevity

& compare that number to the depth (in feet)
of Novosibirsk oil pits & the length of tarred feathers

from now extinct birds. Hold an antenna
into the blizzard-air & count the wing beats

of a Cold War helicopter. Then stare
into soup, a lunch of stones & floor sweepings,

& compose a Trojan Horse blueprint
from the sawdust lining your bowl. Pine

for cabbage, then sculpt with a rusted butter
knife the image of a grander pining: Helen

or Athena. Whittle that face down to strands
of stars. From the density of each

star's light, guess its distance from earth,
how long it takes to arrive, & why.

From Winslow Homer's Ocean, a Nation

—based on "The Fog Warning"

Each American, the painter believed,
was a rowboat, a speck lost in the cosmos.

Collected, however, we were gathering
waves: a repetitive brutality.
                    And here was gray-
blue fog ready to shroud it all Behind the painter's back,

the nineteenth century—like all centuries—
was shredding its occupants: each Civil War soul
was reeled into the clouds—
                    or so we had hoped
while corpses pyramided plots of farmland.

Because each half-mast flag would become
crushed by a mountain of footnotes.
Because the footnotes' authors, as they write,
will crush themselves

the painter refused,
even as dusk glistened his retinas,
to make a slice
                    where sun & water touch.

Newfoundland

fishermen thread copper into microchips the ocean
develops cod into negatives scattered on the shore as
if on the floor of a red one room shack nailed up
rotting tuckamores stunted more daily by wind rain
when not snow the sun making a guest appearance
on the mainland fishermen clapping when the
factories open fishermen clapping when the factories
close rather patrol the shoreline great white whales
breaching the poverty of mollusks & kelp browning
in the snow no one knows but the ocean freezes over
no one knows but the icebergs grieve for each boat
they toss aside fishermen fold cardboard into boxes
the fishermen fold

On Two Paintings by Thomas Eakins

—inspired by "Biglin Brothers Racing" and "The Swimming Hole"

Exactitude of tricep, extended, strained:
your rowers caught mid-motion. Hue of the skin,
late day's pale light on water—each minutiae
gridded & plotted, no deviation, the pain

on the sculler's face is science. The same patterns that
made a body human, you claimed,
were found inside the clockworks of our nation:
money & law, thank God, were limbs of Darwin.

You praised your era, but that era loathed
your steadfast bluntness: young men unclothed,
diving into a pond, a finger reaching toward
a buttock—as if that hand could wield a knife

& slice away the aristocracy—Its scorn
made you retreat. Decline became your pose.

Typical Homeland

I ask Miranda if the 5th St. Corridor is still
"a little UN". Her rambling is scathing:
younger brother, jaw-dropped,
from the porch, watched one man
holler, shrink, & bleed beneath five others,
everyone meth thin armed with hammers.
Why don't your folks plow outta there
I want to email back, but I'm tired
of the library. My wife's making pizzas
from scratch—not for artistic flare—
money's so tight it was this or Raman.
Ah, the summer of the blue-collar bred
grad student…Mother still doesn't get it:
aren't you all professors or something?
How to complain when her house is mortgaged
so much it'll take ten lifespans to pay it?
It's frustrating to know
someone whose woes will always trump:
hello, I'd like to be the object
of sympathy here!:
                                    Thank god
for our colleagues.
At a last-minute dinner party
(hooray! meat & booze tonight),
they mourn the kicked-out extras:
no buffalo sans hormone, no wild sockeye.
Only, sad to say, chickens who had a decent life.
On a side note: don't all chickens end up dead,
their headless bodies spurting blood?
Free range is not about the end,
it's about the before:
                                    gin-soaked sanctimony
of our host. But what if before was slogging
through North Philadelphia side streets,
those kaleidoscopes of glass,
& fishing through trash
stained with pigeon shit? *Then that end*
is a mere, welcomed reprieve,

my wife huffs later, *you're too drunk,*
good night…
                    She's right. I want to puke
standing in my boxers (*you'll wear anything*
until it just falls off) outside,
my thin strip of garden, the bougainvilleas
about to flower, about to die,
it's all on me.

Our Father

was a whipped mule, lathered hard.

He fell into the evening
the way the mugged hug the mugger.

He circled us with a smashed plate
& asked us to forgive him...

We stared at our feet awhile.
They looked like boats we could sail

into another century. But no,
we played blackjack with our hearts

as he leaned against our doors,
cup to ear, afterwards, to listen.

Soon we learned to veil ourselves
from ourselves, deaf

to the approaching siren's wail
as though our stick-thick

bodies could not sink
in our backyard, leaf-strewn pool.

From One Depressive to Another

Irreversible cliché, Frank...
—Thomas Lux, "Elegy for Frank Stafford"

The psychiatrist, an interviewee on "Fresh Air,"
tells the public what we long knew
about ourselves: it's like trying to speak
from a hole, & the more we do the more dirt
crumbles atop our heads, & the further
in the ground we are lowered...

People talk to us & they don't
understand our *unique* dread,
a dread so enormously boring
it rolls out past the interstate

to this, as the brochure proclaims, rest-chalet
pinned in by pinyon & cypress, the mountains
behind looming like crazy seminarians.
Herr Doctor to your right, father left,
the two flags of your future waving brazenly.

My darling, you gave them a show.
My darling, the "vitamin-filled" needles are applauding.
My darling, you broke our contract:

the ones like us hold out the wrist,
& trembling, drop the butter knife,
or swallow half a box of Unisom
as practice for the inevitable. But when
that hooded-figure whips its horse
with the scythe's grainy stem...

My darling, you broke.

Soap Woman

Adipocere: that's what her fat, muscle, tissue,
each inch of her, once ravaged by yellow fever, hardened
into. You,
for the meager price of five dollars, can drag
our hand along the bullet proof glass
or push the button to see the x-ray
of what she ingested
over her brief life: pins, nails, needles—
accoutrements that have no business
being inside us. You can't

touch her: the acid in your fingertips,
silent decomposer. Most people
mull around the exhibit two to three minutes,
occasionally glancing up (the corpse
is waist-high) & shivering
at photos of late-stage syphilitics
whose scab-ridden faces collapsed
unceremoniously—How mortifying

it must have been
to announce to one's neighbors,
city, country, world, look at me
I had sex the wrong way! At the end,
death must have been a welcomed
reprieve. No such luck for Soap Woman:
in 30 watt light, against the stiff
warnings adorning the entries & exits,
among the amblers & the nauseated
someone always zooms the lens
& snaps her mummified mouth
forever molded in a scream.

Contest

I raised my hand to the venetian-blinds
& looked the way a doctor would an X-ray.

Meanwhile the girl who called me up
lay at my feet with a fist-sized hole in her head.

If blood were a sea, I should've dove into it
as some stretch of sky would be touched by fire.

Why I'm telling you this, dear reader, now
twelve years after the fact, has little to do with need

for company or profundity or skill.
I want you to forgive me

with the boldness of conviction
or something even less likely to change,

although what that is is beyond me.
I take your time, your attention, with selfishness

I suppose, & what have I given you yet?
I would like to offer this river X, an indecipherable body

you may cut with long smooth strokes or small ones.
Its affection will rise to its clear surface like oxygen.

It shall remember you—Graceful, intact, a winner.

Girl Says I

was not the horse, lathered & fagged, dipping its mouth for drink

nor the river, the heavy noxious brown, the knee-deep murk

nor the swaying half-sawed elms, branches drooped & pollen-heavy

nor the stumbling mid-air bee, its hum-brake-hum, one wing severed

nor the severing, the cleaver's cherry handle, the cattle's flank grilling

nor the fire, nor the wood, nor the sparks flicking upon shadowed faces

nor the face, smallpox-scarred, a tooth remaining then lost in sleep

nor the sleep, the valley's children, miniature hands mallets in dream

nor the dream, the ease of flying, the mountains breasts, peaks nipples

nor the snow, the nipple's milk, the river below, its gurgled language

nor the language, the him-haw pleading, the take-me-back, the one-
time-night,

the never-again, the never, the nor

We were Fourteen & Drifting

Into our fathers. We were lopsided boats
Swallowed by the horizon. Porn was, yawn,
Porn by now, but who would've guessed
This: a woman in a tent-sized wedding dress
Giving the time to a chestnut-eyed Palomino.
I want to think she's enjoying it but I know she's not.
I want to know if she's that hard up for drugs.
I want the horse's opinion on all of this...
He's probably in a first grader's art kit,
And she, if lucky, lugs an anvil of embarrassment.
Today, I lug my own luggage out
Into the bright light of responsibility, & find
My love with open arms. I want to know
The secret formulas of the electric bill,
The finesse it takes to buy the freshest milk.
Lord, please allow my curiosity to be used
For only honorable endeavors that I can ride
Across the flat landscape where regret gets
Enveloped in the neck high grass, & all the men,
Old by now, are asleep on their porches,
Part of their contrition. Let my gaze
Penetrate my love deep into her mouth,
In the crevices where desperation mixes
With her spit, where words often are
Masticated, & let my tongue trace each harsh
Cell of inner cheek, each inch a river
To be blessed with sun, & let that sun arch
Across each human: the woman about to be
Punched in her face, the cameraman
Throwing a fit, the owner kicking his animal—
Let the sun arch & obliterate all of this,
Until we rise from the heat like zebras
Zipping away from the lion, the lion getting
Gaunter, gaunter,
                    I never want to be my father.

Plymouth, Montserrat, 1996

Neck-deep, mud & ash, Dante.

Palms center-split. Pumice boulders car-sized.
The airplanes can't lift away quick enough.

Once in the air, someone in a tropical
shirt thinks *well, that's the end of that drama.*

The island's a beach the size of a fingernail.

Lava's a cell on the earth's tongue:

a horseshoe crab scurries sideways
between two scorched time-shares,

& does his little dance.

Diary Excerpt of a Laid-Off Philadelphia Ferry Worker, Circa 1930

I once gazed upon the river & thought it was the sea:
New Jersey was not visible—the fog was thick, the air
lined with ice—& I heard women talk of pulling their
shawls tighter & of the little puffs of steam from their
mouths. I could smell the factory waste my boat
parted, & I, for a moment, turned & saw those people
behind my back: their faces were red & swollen &
wet. Was this what we added up to? Where I live now,
there are fleets of alley dogs, fur matted & twisted, &
sometimes someone throws a ham shank, & then the
fight is on. The men are boys & the boys are boys &
they all slap their knees & guffaw as the dogs twitch
on the ground & the shank lays untouched & dotted
with blood. I used to think the human heart was
something of a vault & all we had to do was look
inward to withdraw from it. Now, the heart is still a
vault, but the bank in which it's encased is just so
much paper lining the floors, so much dust in the air.
It makes you want to tie an anchor to your feet. It
makes you want to take a poker to your wife, & she to
you. But sometimes she & I walk by the river, & an
old man is selling apples. I buy one & hand it to her.
On the opposing bank, there's one small glint of light,
from where we do not know, & that, I dream, is where
we're going.

III.

Pool Party

When the stars revealed their shamelessness, everyone got naked.

The fat ones, like me, bobbed along the water.
The better ones stood knee-deep, the pool lights illuminating
Their remarkable posteriors. A Bulgarian leapt off
The diving board, uncircumcised & vulnerable in the air.
The German toddlers wandered about

Ignorant of our aberrations. Steaks were sizzling
Behind us. Everyone was laughing
As though that couple wouldn't start

Thrusting in front of us, their mangled shapes
Breaking the chlorinated calm.

One Night, Like Always Lately, Before Bed

I mean to say these nights
in my new studio, which are quiet & everything
I had said I wanted. But they've mutated
into a mattress of hours, I'm left to ponder
darkened, stucco stars. If I avert gazing
at the ceiling's galaxy, & flip
to the left, there's a red dot hollering
across the barely moonlit room: FM Stereo
Indicator assuring me I can't miss DJ Dog
going apeshit on a caller, a troglodyte
insomniac who stutters five seconds of fame.
Really, it's sickening, but I've swallowed
two Valium, although nothing tonight
will rock me toward sleep. I've fallen in love

with my stomach's acid, churning like a gear
in a sawmill: there was my wife
slashing my face. Nothing to say to save us
in that apartment's jaundiced light,
even the car couldn't take me
away from myself. Now its dog-eared registration
lies buried in my oak dresser drawer
beneath a postcard of cabins in a valley of snow
where each yard is filled with firewood,
& beyond those piles, a floor of pine needles
atop a glazed white, & above that floor,
branches sighing with ice. On one arm-
thick branch, an eviscerated deer dangles,

its body cleansed out of the stride
that pushed it forward, & the misery it felt
when that stride was shot short.
When I look back now—when I look forward
palm fronds sizzle in a fire-colored dawn,
boulevards echo an unscrupulous night life
that parks its stolen cars under a busted street light,
& in the darkness, falls silent, before revealing
faces via a flash of flame. In a minute, a chorus

of doors will creak, the stars above will blaze,
& in the last seconds of life, I will tense
my pectorals, puff my cigarette, & laugh.

On Jasper Johns' Targets

The picket fence, the fintailed roadster,
the TV dinner, *Leave it to Beaver*—
these are the target's peripheries. Dead
center is us, vanishing point, our dread

exemplified by his busy brushwork. Where's
the half-shadowed lakes, the spread
of background trees, his critics complained,
where's the art? Black ash in the air

would be Johns' reply, if he weren't so cool.
He wore indifference like a well-made robe
the aging playboy sports besides the pool.
If the world is to end, better to be luscious

than panicked, playfully spinning the globe
on a finger, half-cocked grin of a fool.

Supreme Court Makes Pact to Lose Virginity by the End of December 2002

We were so busy making laws we forgot to make
it with each other. Our blacks robes blackened
the fire smoldering in our loins. That changed

when all those jock Senators, the football players
who often cartwheeled the cheerleaders,
tossed eggs in our direction & started to guffaw.

How little we were, shot down off our marble
podiums; we once stood above the country
like a ranger on fire look out. And for what save

your nights when the fathers step from the adult
bookstores blinking their filth like a promise,
& when the mothers rock themselves to sleep.

When you see us towering over the news
correspondents, redwoods stretching toward
the sun like your hearts, think of us asking

each other *what's that on your soda can;*
it looks like a hair, but these days we see
anything to appear less alone.

Grimace

Gumdrop, monster, abused
pear? All I know is his
purpleness worn like a gaudy dress. He cha-chas

next to a semi-obese celebrity, both holding cheeseburgers
above their heads as if torches emblazoning
the night. But a gumdrop

is 1/1000 of his mass, a pear 1.5%:
the blubber world's strange mathematics,
give me your tired, your hungry...your more

hungry. A crude friend

called last night: *dude go to the McDonald's*
webpage, & there it was:

he's Ronald's best friend & will do anything to get a cheeseburger.
A gumdrop during midnight below a streetlight on a corner,

fishnets: that's why we call him Grimace.

Prisons of Grace: So Much for Novelty

On the court, the great leapers are applauded.
Popcorn like rose petals is tossed at their feet.

In the court, the great leapers are examined.
For hours, a flaxen pubic hair, or the denial of it,

Is whipped upon their narratives: Xerxes & the shore:
Each apology a sand grain: try to count the stutters

As the flashbulbs sail to new, round rumps of land
With infinite forests of rape kits, marshes of syphilis,

Where the golden dusk dies the same each night.
So why, my little Columbus, shall we speak of it?

Middle Class Syphilis

It happens to other fraternities. It was definitely the toilet seat. It was her pajamas embroidered with silk suns but patchwork nimbus. It was the nimbus settling over our heads to prove a point. It was the hard burn of whiskey. It was the children she spoke of like future ambitions. It was the new minivan of 2018. It was moiling around with another in its back seat. It was bacteria that glittered like stock options. They were the type of options whose light reached you once the source had long died. The sources were the type of sources that begged to be classified. Today one ad said, runs, $1000 OBO. Another said brilliant, fashionable, thin, muscled, IQ 150, saw you over the meat rack, liked your rack, hazel eyes, blond hair, no freaks, no sickos, likes to toss salad, donkey punch, be beaten, swap, swing, OBO.

Panning

I once abhorred the ex-marine on TV
who hooked up his daughter's beaus to lie detectors.

They stuttered like caught schoolboys because they were
competing for her hand—perfect as sculpture—& cash.

She or her less glamorous twin was found today
facedown in a swimming pool. It was so new

there wasn't even water yet—it made the splayed corpse
more vulgar, as though if she floated, her body

would appear at leisure. In the sun,
as it were, she was craned out. The ex-marine raised

his hand to his bulbous, swollen face, choking
in front of the cameras, blinded by the hot white light,

& sobbing why, good god why,
are you taping this?

Your Tendermost Feelings Etched in Stone

—Ad in *SkyMall* magazine

Finally, my wife doesn't have to die
in order for my sentiment to live on.

No, she goes about her day preparing
tax forms or burping the baby & there it is:

her miniature slab beside the alarm clock.
Once, there was only a picture of us,

younger, cheek-to-cheek, a waterfall raging
in the background. You can't notice it

but our faces are pulled taut, stressed,
a comment I made about permanence,

ebb & flow. We hiked four miles up
an abandoned mine road at 10,000 feet

so I could say that. Only if she had had this
stone. Perhaps I could have looked & felt

the type of eternalness silence breeds.
Perhaps my heart would've leapt

from its meager cage of bone. As it were,
the fir trees swung back & forth.

The last of the snow hung
on the mountain, as if the mountain despised it

& relished its despising. I'm beginning
to feel my lack take on a physicality

I could hold in my hand, & like David,
the world's stretched back, & it flies.

28

This is the beginning of the downhill that everyone says
      is the downhill,

& see that lemon, that's my prostate, & I postulate

by the time it rolls down to that exceptionally fuzzy willow on that
      hump on the hill's reprieve,

it shall swell to a radio. It shall receive NPR. Or Sports Talk. Something
      with a voice, either measured or fluctuating

on the spectrum from *Angry* to *Going To Put My Kid Through the
      Dashboard*.

It seems all my contemporaries talk of children. But I am a
      contemporary, with a plan, a book

whose glossy cover reads *HEAL!!*, & a pen whose ink
      is my mother's blood

that smells of olive oil & the sea—Italy!

Anyone who is important must go there, with its streets
      as wide as string cheese, its tightly-wound rotaries

where refrigerator boxes masquerade as cars.

But I'm afraid to fly

these days, I tell my wife. She tells me these days

what looks like the downhill may really be the uphill,
      & what is up must—

Subjunctive

If I were a lesion, I would ask to grow in the space
between light & no light, touch & the memory of
touch—made before the monks' pre-dawn vespers,
one meager reading lamp upon the words changing
into sound, & if that sound were to stretch across the
flat land, scarcely visible from the highway, & in the
winter the brown snow upon the bull's swollen
hooves did not melt, does not grow, was not, is—

The Sameness of Animals

We observed miles of mango
lassies, pyramids of Basmati
rice, the lively chatter of Punjabi

celebrating some festival
of rebirth. An ox or cow skull
would fall into the Ganges,

& by the miracle of its own
divinity, returned as a strapping
calf. How holy can an animal be

if the others can't know
which grazing is sustenance,
which indiscretion? When a cow

strolls down to a stream,
& gulps a swatch of muddy brown
water, the carp swing wildly left

to avoid those thick, black lips.
They do so because they fear
everything, & perhaps this is

the right approach. A friend says
your new home abuts a wharf
where fish are brought to dry

before they are boxed,
tagged, & sent to our cities
where cages rattle over

restaurant doors before
the waiters wave good night,
slip into cars, & become

other beings.

On Other Planets

the starlight cuts through the heart

like a hot knife through butter,

except when the willows & elms

collect this light first, store it

in their leaves, wait for the rain

to rain down, & when that rain explodes

the ground, light each thumbnail-

thick drop until a thousand drops

are a thousand beacons

luring the ominous, glowing eyes

out of the bushes—

each animal identifies itself,

sits around a pond as though around

a prayer circle, joins paws when one

tiger or wolf says *Forgive me for eating*

your mother, your children, your friends

& the pond water rises up, one enormous

geyser, & beneath, a yellow orb of heat

so strong you'd swear this world was scorched

to its ends, but then the water falls

back down, extinguishes the light,

& the animals stretch their paws,

settle down for the night.

Very Minor Elegies

To whom would I show my superfluous nipple?
Would one kiss it as if the ring upon a great pontiff's
finger? I'm quite worried these days about John Paul,
his wobbling over The Word as if an exclamation in
Matthew could crumble his ribs. He might rejoice in
joining Our Maker, but the rest of us are stuck looking
at the same stars each night in a slightly different
position. Today, I told myself *you dreamed of roughing
it under the stars.* Change has always rumpled me. I
see each new calendar as a loan shark's thug twisting
back my arms. My body, in silent increments, has
grown tired of this behavior. The great bangs of youth
bid well to my sloping forehead. One morning, I'll
look in the obituaries and say *now, that was a handsome
man. Wait a minute. Fuck.*

I & We

The buses weren't running that night.
The planes had been grounded by the snow.
Even the taxi cabs slept inside the frigid wombs

of their garages. I had these two legs
but my quadriceps were on the verge of buckling
from the knee-deep drifts. All that remained was

the 24/7 coffee shop where vagrant,
after-party Navy men took pensive sips of Sanka
as if drinking their inscrutable, black hearts.

I walked through the door whereupon
bells jangled, my presence so important
I had to be announced. Yet, I leaned against

the cash register larger than a coffin,
& watched one woman, a knit cap on her head
whose yarn was unraveling like centuries,

recite passages from the bible in the tones
of someone hanging on the cross
of what she forgot or what would never arrive,

& it bored her. I stood for a long time,
so long in fact my stillness seemed a motion
& the snow outside the static, & this flock

of saints, my newly ordained family,
cantankerous quarks about to implode.

I Was a Finalist

for wife ignorer of the year, for fat-man-in-too-tight-
dress-shirt becomes ninth-grade laughingstock,
for pet obsesser of Vega County. I was chosen

for the snoring-decibel championships,
for open your mouth & count the cavities,
for man most likely not to have a bust

made after him. I was honored by the humane
societies of northern Maine for my long mane,
by both the Mustard Association of New Mexico

& the Anti-Onion League for my breath. I was regaled
by oldsters whose hips are sturdier than mine,
whose jokes echo across the sea like sonar,

& I became the joking envy of dolphins for my sleek
yet out-of-place dorsal fin. I breezed through
England's cheese shops, made light of Normandy's

infinite wineries—my bulbous made the grapes
jealous. I made the Great Wall come down,
the Berlin Wall re-erect, the Coke bottle on the villager

fall again from the African sky. I was the Coke bottle.
I was the savanna. I was the river near
the Coke bottle on the savanna from which a tiger

mauled some rare breed of antelope. I was the monkey
that watched the mauling, the brush plant that cared
nothing about it, the sun bored with my sunness,

the one lone nimbus. I was the sky, the sheet
simile for the sky, where death was a mere veil,
but I was never its bridesmaid, never its bride.

Notes

"A Half-Century Contemplating the Double Helix": The title was a headline for a story on National Public Radio's *All Things Considered*.

"If One is Wise He is a Traveler…": Title is a quote from Seneca.

"Grimace": In the unlikely event someone from McDonald's reads this manuscript, I can not prove that I actually found this quote about Grimace on the company website, although it sticks in my memory as being painfully true.

"From One to Depressive to Another": For J.S.

"Soap Woman": An exhibit about Soap Woman can be found at the Mutters Museum in Philadelphia, PA—a museum dedicated to the evolution of American medicine and medical oddities.

"Supreme Court…": Title came from *The Onion*.

"The Sameness of Animals": For A.S.

"Very Minor Elegies": Respectfully draws its influence from W.S. Merwin's "Elegy".

"I & We": Inspired by Buber's *I & Thou*.

Joseph P. Wood is the author of five chapbooks and another forthcoming collection of poetry, *Fold of the Map* (Salmon Poetry Ltd.) He has published in a variety of journals that include *BOMB, Boston Review, Gulf Coast, Hunger Mountain, Indiana Review, Prairie Schooner, Verse,* and *West Branch,* among others. He is co-founder of Slash Pine Press and director of the Slash Pine Poetry Festival. He, his wife, and daughter live in Tuscaloosa, AL.

LaVergne, TN USA
05 March 2011
218975LV00002B/29/P